Nelle Harper Lee

Master Storyteller

Roz Morris

Seacoast Publishing
Birmingham, Alabama

Published by Seacoast Publishing, Inc.
1149 Mountain Oaks Drive
Birmingham, Alabama 35226

Library of Congress Control Number: 2007938043
Cover art by Thomas B. Moore

ISBN 1-59421-040-3

To obtain copies of this book, please write or call:
Seacoast Publishing, Inc.
Post Office Box 26492
Birmingham, Alabama 35260
(205) 979-2909

About The Series

Alabama Roots is a book series designed to provide reading pleasure for young people, to allow readers to better know the men and women who shaped the State of Alabama, and to fill a much-needed void of quality regional non-fiction for students in middle grades.

For years, teachers and librarians have searched for quality biographies about famous people from Alabama. This series is a response to that search. The series will cover a span of time from pre-statehood through the modern day.

The goal of *Alabama Roots* is to provide biographies that are historically accurate and as interesting as the characters whose lives they explore.

The *Alabama Roots* mark assures readers and educators of consistent quality in research, composition, and presentation.

It is a joint publishing project of Seacoast Publishing, Inc., and Will Publishing, Inc., both located in Birmingham, Alabama.

Dedication

"Mockingbirds don't do one thing but make music for us to enjoy . . . but sing their hearts out for us. That's why it's a sin to kill a mockingbird."

To my middle child, Abby Morris Allen, the one with the tender heart that has always made music in our lives. Remember that sometimes last can be best. This one is for you, Abby.

Nelle Harper Lee

Researching Harper Lee

There is an astonishing amount of interest in the life of Harper Lee. Typing her name into a Google search on the Internet provides more than 3,000,000 hits. However, much of the information provided on these sites has not been verified or documented. So, using the Internet for research purposes had to be done carefully. Only stories and interviews that could be documented in other ways could be used. It was a monumental task to try to weed through many of these accounts.

In May 2006, I contacted Ms. Lee to see if she would be interested in participating in our *Alabama Roots* project to write her biography. As with most other requests for interviews and public appearances, Ms. Lee politely declined. She did suggest that if I continued with the project that I not use Charles Shields' recently published *Mockingbird* as suitable research material because it contained many "errors of fact and plain untruths." So, when I read *Mockingbird* and stories that it included, I again had to go back and find other ways to prove that these stories had actually happened.

I made several visits to the Birmingham Public Library as well as to the University of Alabama Southern History Library. These visits provided interview information as well as a few letters written by Ms. Lee.

The most fun part of this research project, though, was my visits to Monroeville, Alabama. I first visited on a scorching June day in 2006. I gathered all of the pamphlets and materials offered at the Monroe County Heritage Museums, and even though the temperature was well over 90 degrees, I took the *Monroeville in the 1930s Walking Tour*. It was a dreamlike experience to stand inside the courtroom of the courthouse because this courtroom was used as the model for the one in the movie *To Kill a Mockingbird*.

I visited the United Methodist Church cemetery and found the graves of Harper Lee's parents and brother. However, even though this trip was great fun and further sparked my interest in this book, I gathered little research material that I could use.

Then, on June 28, 2007, a full year later, I finally hit my lucky break. By this point, I had written a rough draft trying to verify that all of my stories and accounts were true and accurate. On this day, I visited the Monroe County Heritage Museums once again. Later that afternoon, I had one of my favorite interviews that I have ever done. I visited with Jennings Faulk Carter, cousin of Truman Capote and childhood friend of Nelle Harper Lee. It is such a tribute to Harper Lee that her friends and townspeople so carefully respect her requested privacy. Both the museum director and Mr. Carter made sure that nothing was told that would be offensive to Harper Lee. Mr. Carter agreed to read a copy of my rough draft and correct any errors of fact that he found. Since a large part of the book is childhood stories, I felt good about him letting me know if I got that part right.

It would still be my greatest dream to sit down and visit with Harper Lee to discuss her life, but that doesn't seem as though it will happen. It is my desire that the account of her life that I have put together is as fair and accurate as she would want it to be. Alabama school teachers made Harper Lee the number one most requested book for the *Alabama Roots* series. I hope this book has been worth the wait!

Roz Morris

To Kill a Mockingbird

The book, *To Kill a Mockingbird*, is an American classic. The story takes place in the fictional town of Maycomb, Alabama in the 1930s. It is told by the main character, Jean Louise "Scout" Finch. Her father, Atticus Finch, is a lawyer.

Atticus takes on a law case defending a black man named Tom Robinson. Atticus knows that Tom is innocent. He also knows that Tom doesn't stand much of a chance of being set free. He knows that no white jury in the 1930s in Alabama would believe a black man over the white woman who was to testify against him. Because Atticus is defending a black man, Scout and Jem get made fun of, have trouble keeping their tempers and are almost hurt. But one of their unusual neighbors saves Scout from harm.

The book's title comes from something that Atticus says to his children. He tells them "It's a sin to kill a mockingbird."

The Jefferson County Library Cooperative (JCLC) named *To Kill a Mockingbird* as their "One County-One Book" program for the 2008 school year. The goal is to get thousands of people throughout the state of Alabama to read this book.

Prologue

MONROEVILLE IS A SLOW, sleepy town in southwestern Alabama. Lying about one hundred miles south of Montgomery off U.S. 84, its sandy land and piney woods are dotted by old homes where people have lived all of their lives never feeling the need for anything different.

It could be just like other small Alabama towns, but it isn't.

It might look the same as other small towns, but it is different.

That difference is best seen each year when the Old Courthouse Museum becomes a theater. Beginning each spring, an all-local theater group performs a two-act play based on a book written by one of Monroeville's townspeople. The first act is performed on the back lawn while the second act is upstairs in the oval courtroom.

As with many small southern towns, in the center of the square lies the Monroe County Courthouse. A small professionally printed sign states simply, "Do Not

Break Camellias" as the huge bushes hang dotted with brightly colored flowers in cool weather. The courthouse is always open to the public, including the beautiful courtroom. Today, it is home for the Monroe County Heritage Museums. Sunlight splashes through the double set of tall lean windows onto rows of wooden benches much like church pews. A beautiful tin ceiling dotted with patterns of dogwood blooms can be admired from the third floor balcony. A shiny pressed native gum floor leads to the judge's bench in the front of the courtroom. A jury box lies to the judge's right.

In 1903, Judge Nicholas Stallworth decided that Monroeville was "the hub of Southwestern Alabama" and needed a dignified courthouse to show this position. Building began and troubles quickly followed. The architect lost his plans and new ones had to be made. Once construction got underway, planners realized that no one had told the workers to dig a basement. The huge brick four-storied building kept costing more and more to build.

When time came for the next election, voters thought about this costly project and nicknamed the courthouse "Stallworth's Folly." Judge Stallworth was not reelected, but his dream building was finished.

In the late 1920s, during the Great Depression, a

time when few in the South had any money to spare, this town gave an eager young girl and boy plenty to explore and later much to write about. One of the little girl's favorite pastimes was to climb into the third floor balcony of the beautiful courtroom to watch her father doing his job as a lawyer. The boy who tagged along with her later complained that sometimes it seemed that all his playmate wanted to do was "hang around at the courthouse and play golf."

Yet, this courthouse and this town fed the minds and imaginations of these two children. Both later became world-known writers. Truman Streckfus Persons later changed his name to Truman Capote and became famous as an outstanding writer. His childhood playmate did too. Using the idea that she should write about what she knew, the grown-up young lady wrote a story based on this town and this courthouse. The book was called *To Kill A Mockingbird*. It has sold more than 30 million copies worldwide and its shy, down-to-earth author still lives a large part of the year in Monroeville.

Her name is Nelle Harper Lee and this is her story.

Chapter 1

AMASA COLEMAN LEE was born on July 19, 1880 in Georgiana, Alabama, a little railroad town 50 miles southwest of Montgomery.

He was born just about in the middle of eight brothers and sisters to Methodist parents who were strong in their faith. No drinking, card playing or other wasteful activities for the Lee family.

Everyone called him Coley, and soon enough assigned him more than enough farm chores that he had no time for wasteful activities.

Even though he never had much time for school and learning, he was an exceptionally bright boy. In fact, Coley decided that he wanted to be a teacher and passed the teacher's exam at age sixteen. He set out for Marianna, Florida where he taught for three years. When he found the teaching job, Coley thought "A.C." sounded more proper, so that was how he began to introduce himself.

A.C. wanted to advance in life, and teaching

wasn't offering him the money that he needed. So, he found a job as bookkeeper at Flat Creek Mill in Finchburg, Alabama, a little town near the border of Monroe and Clarke counties.

Once A.C. got settled, of course, he had to find a church to attend.

"Why don't you visit in my church this weekend, young man?" Finch suggested.

"I'd be glad to, sir," A.C. quickly replied.

That Sunday morning, A.C. met the Finch's daughter, Frances. A.C. was impressed. Frances played the piano, sang, and was considered quite an artist. A.C. saw right away that she had an excellent education.

"Where did you attend school?" A.C. asked.

Frances smiled her gentle, quiet smile. "My sister, Alice, and I both attended the new Alabama Girls' Industrial School once we turned fifteen years old. Have you heard of the school?"

A.C. shook his head *no.*

"It was started by Miss Julia Tutwiler in 1892," Frances explained. "You can't imagine all of the classes that were offered. Why, there was stenography, photography, sewing, cooking, dressmaking, and home nursing," Frances ticked off on her fingers.

A.C. was impressed, so impressed that he soon asked Frances to marry him. The wedding was in her parents' home on June 22, 1910. A.C. was thirty years old. Frances was only nineteen. A.C. knew that Frances wanted a cultured life. So, in 1912, he moved his wife and baby girl, Alice, to Monroeville, Alabama.

A.C. hoped things were beginning to grow in this town of 700. The Manistee and Repton Railroad laid tracks through downtown Monroeville. A.C. became the financial manager for the law firm Barnett & Bugg, which took care of the railroad's business. By 1915, A.C. earned his own law degree and became a partner in the "new firm" of Barnett, Bugg and Lee.

Soon, the beautiful Monroe County courthouse was framed by brick buildings, a sign of promise for a better future. The Lees noticed the town's growth, and saw it as a good sign. Daughter Alice was joined by a sister, Frances Louise, in 1916. Then, in 1920, the Lee family added a son, Edwin Coleman Lee.

In 1918, the United States was fighting World War I, a conflict in which soldiers were dying from poison gas attacks and terrible bombardments. A.C. frightened Frances when he announced, "I am going to register for the draft. Even though I am thirty-eight years old, our American troops are suffering terrible losses in this world war that is going on. It is my duty."

Even though Alice was only a small child, she later recalled, "I remember the anxiety among adults when it looked as though married men with dependents were facing the draft."

Both Alice and her mother drew a sigh of relief when the war ended that November. A.C. would not be a soldier after all.

Life returned to its routine. A.C. worked for the law firm. The Lee children played and entertained themselves in this friendly southern town. Louise, known as "Weezie", was thought of as the "pretty one." Alice was small, birdlike and full of humor. The family called her "Bear." Edwin was a quiet boy. Everyone just called him *Brother.*

A.C.'s career was growing along with the family. In 1926, he ran for the state Legislature as a Democrat and won. More importantly, on April 28, the family welcomed a new baby. Frances had a wonderful idea for her name. "Let's take her Grandmother Ellen's name and spell it backward," she suggested. "We can name her Nelle." But they didn't call her that. Instead, they called her *Dody.*

As her daughter grew older, Frances realized that she and this youngest child were totally different. While everyone thought of Frances as quiet and gentle, little Dody quickly became a tomboy who climbed trees, threw rocks, and bossed other children around.

Little Dody and trouble became good friends.

Chapter 2

"SHE WAS JUST LIKE A BOY!" remembered Taylor Faircloth of Nelle's summer vacation days at her Aunt Alice's house in Atmore, Alabama. "She would come down and stay sometimes three or four weeks in the summer.

"In a small town, everybody knew everybody, and we just kind of roamed around like wild animals. We had no boundaries. She got rid of all her surplus hair in the summertime, and she could climb tall trees. When we played 'capture the flag' at night, she held on longer than anybody."

Nelle loved those visits to her Aunt Alice's house because it gave her somebody new to play with. Back at home, her sister Alice was grown up and working by the time Dody was old enough to play. Louise stayed busy with her social life in 4-H and youth activities at Monroeville Methodist Episcopal Church. Edwin, or 'Brother', sometimes played with Dody when he was home, but many days, he preferred to be alone and Dody had nothing to do.

No other young girls lived on her block of South Alabama Avenue. One time a little girl moved in across the street, but her family stayed only a little while. Dody spent some of her time spying on her old neighbors further down the street. Yet, she had to keep her distance while doing so.

"Dody, don't you go bothering Captain and Mrs. Jones," A.C. cautioned. ""You know that she is in a wheelchair and doesn't feel well."

Captain Powell Jones, a former Confederate soldier, and his wife often sat on the front porch of their house. Sitting in her wheelchair, Mrs. Jones hounded her poor husband, fussing and fretting over every little thing. He wasn't her only victim, though. Any children who passed by the house would get an earful of her complaints.

"Girl, you need to get out of those overalls and clean yourself up!" she'd shout as Nelle passed by. As a child, though, spying on neighbors got boring pretty fast. If Nelle headed away from town, the neighbors were Mr. and Mrs. Hendrix, a druggist and his wife. All of their children were grown, so they didn't offer much entertainment for little Nelle. It was no wonder that she looked forward to going to school. As rough and tumble as she was on the playground, she was very smart in school. She knew more words than most of the other children, probably because at home she'd sit on A.C.'s lap to "help" him read the newspaper or solve a crossword puzzle.

School was a confusing place for Nelle, though. One of her teachers was Mrs. Leighton McNeil. Mrs. McNeil traveled ten miles every morning on dusty dirt roads from Frisco City to teach her class. On the first day of school, she introduced herself to the children and told them what to expect in her class.

Nelle politely raised her hand.

"Yes, Nelle?" asked Mrs. McNeil.

"Leighton, I was wondering when we get to go outside to play?" Nelle asked as she eagerly looked around at new playmates.

One of Nelle's classmates, Freda Roberson, turned around in her desk and gasped as this impolite girl who had just called their teacher by her first name. *Who does she think she is?* wondered Freda.

Quickly, Mrs. McNeil scolded her. "Nelle, you are a small child, a student in my class. You may not greet me by my first name."

Nelle was totally confused. "Ma'am, I don't understand."

"What do you mean you don't understand?" asked the teacher. "It is improper for a child to address an adult by their first name."

"At home, I call my father by his first name," Nelle calmly explained.

Freda wondered what kind of home Nelle came from.

Nelle was a force to be reckoned with on the playground, too. One day she was involved in a game of ball with the other children. She played to win. As she was running to first base, she plowed over a little girl, tearing the girl's dress.

"Nelle Lee, you are a bully! You think you know more than anybody else," the little girl shouted angrily.

Other parts of school were too rigid and organized for Nelle.

Her sister, Alice, later said, "Anyone who knows her well will tell you that she is a very highly individualistic person. Nelle was extremely bored by part of the school curriculum."

"One year, there was an agricultural parade, in which schoolchildren were dressed up to represent products of the county," Mrs. Jane Hybart Rosborough recalled. "I wore a fertilizer sack and wasn't happy about it. My friend Sara Anne McCall was a ham." Later, Nelle would use this school event in her book.

Nelle's mother, "Miss Fanny" often suffered from illnesses. It seemed as if she'd never adjusted to life in the small town of Monroeville. Often times, she spent the entire night playing the piano or reading. She could be withdrawn from all of her family and neighbors. She might even act as if she didn't know passersby and wouldn't respond to their greetings. Other times, she might shout out orders to people passing by on the street. It was so confusing for little Dody to know how to react to her mother.

Miss Fanny had help to run her house. Hattie Belle Clausell came over every day to South Alabama Avenue from her home in the "Negro part of town." Everyone called her Hattie Belle. She kept the house clean and tried to keep little Dody straight.

After playing outside and romping around all day long, Dody would hear Hattie Belle call, "Come on, little *Miss Frippy Britches*." It's time for you to get out of them dirty overalls and get ready for supper."

"Let me play a little longer," Dody begged.

"Honey, it's gonna take me a while to get you scrubbed and combed and ready for supper. Now, come on in before your daddy gets home." Hattie Belle always won out and little Dody would be sitting at the table clean and fresh when A.C. came in at the end of the day.

It might have seemed that little Nelle never had any playmates since her brother and sisters were older and busy and since there were no other girls in the neighborhood. That was not the case. When Nelle was almost five years old, she was outside playing in her yard. She climbed up and walked along the low wall that separated her house from the Faulk's house next door. Then, she ambled into her backyard and scrambled up the chinaberry tree to the tree house. From there, she could look down on the neighbor's back yard. On one hot summer day she looked down and saw a strangely-dressed boy strolling through the flower beds in the backyard.

That was Nelle's first real encounter with Truman Streckfus Persons.

It was the beginning of a beautiful and unusual friendship.

Chapter 3

NELLE SAT SILENTLY in her weathered wooden tree house. She idly rubbed one of the twin reddish gray trunks of the chinaberry tree as she watched the odd looking boy in the Faulk's yard next door. Her mind wandered to a conversation she'd heard earlier between her mother and father.

"A.C., I want you to have that old chinaberry tree in the backyard pulled up," Fanny insisted. "All those yellow berries that fall in the yard are a nuisance. The birds spread the seeds all over the yard, and I'm seeing seedlings coming up all over the backyard."

"Fanny, you know what a hard tree that would be to cut down," A.C. gently replied.

Nelle held her breath, silently praying that A.C. wouldn't agree to cut down the tree just to keep her mother happy. Usually, A.C. did anything that he could to make sure that Frances stayed happy and calm.

She heard her father continue, "Let's leave the tree for a few more years. Dody loves that tree house better than anything and since she doesn't have anybody around to play with, it gives her something to do."

"Well, once she's outgrown it, I want that chinaberry tree gone!" Frances demanded.

Nelle kept peering through the long narrow saw-like leaves at the newest victim of her spying.

What an odd little boy! She thought absently.

Down in the Faulk's yard, a fat blond boy walked among the bushes. He looked like he was afraid to get dirty and Nelle could imagine why.

It was the 1930s. America was in the middle of the Great Depression, a time when people had little money to spend on extra things like fine clothes. Yet this little boy was wandering in the yard in a Hawaiian print shirt, white shorts, blue socks, with sandals on his feet. A little white linen cap with a tiny bill perched on his head.

He's what A.C. would describe as a dapper *little boy,* Nelle thought proudly of one of the words she'd learned in one of her word games with her father.

Suddenly, as Nelle stroked one of the small branches, it broke with a snap.

The strange boy looked up and peered through the leaves of the tree.

"Girl, what are you doing up there?" he hollered.

"Are you spying on me?"

"No, I am not!" Nelle replied defiantly. "I'm playing in my tree house."

"Well, come on down here and let me look at you," the boy demanded.

Not used to being bullied, Nelle shot back, "You can't make me."

"No, I can't," the boy calmly replied. "But, I can go inside and tell my Cousin Jenny that some nasty little girl is spying on me."

Nelle scampered down out of the tree. She climbed over the low rock wall that separated her yard from the Faulk's and stomped right up to the boy.

"I'm not nasty!" she shouted as she held up her fists. "You want to fight about it?"

"No, I am not inclined to fight," the lad said in a cultured Yankee tone.

"Who are you, anyway?" Nelle wanted to know.

"My name is Truman Streckfus Persons, but you may call me Truman," said the boy as he stuck out his hand.

Not knowing what else to do, Nelle shook his lily-white hand with her own, dirty and tree-stained as it was.

"I'm here to stay with my Cousins Jenny and Sook for a while," Truman explained. "Who are you and why are you dressed in those overalls?"

"My name is Nelle Harper Lee," Nelle replied. "And, I dress however I darn well please," she added, defiantly sticking out her chin.

Nelle gave the strange boy a long look up and down. Even though he looked so odd, maybe at least he'd be somebody to play with.

"Wanna come up in my tree house?" Nelle asked.

The boy's eyes lit up, but before he could answer Nelle decided, "I guess you'd better not, dressed like that. Why are you dressed up like that in the middle of summer? You goin' to a funeral?"

"No, these are some of the new clothes Jenny bought me," Truman replied.

"You mean she has prissy clothes like that in her hat store?" Nelle asked.

"No, silly!" Truman answered her, ignoring the fact that she called his clothes *prissy*. "Jenny buys my clothes in fine shops in Mobile and Montgomery."

Nelle snorted, "They don't seem like they'd be much fun to play in, though."

Truman's cousins probably weren't thinking about him playing when they bought the fancy clothes. They probably wanted him to have fine things because so many things hadn't been fine in his life so far. Born thirteen months after his mother and father married,

Truman's first few years were spent with his parents regularly fighting and separating from each other. His mother searched for a stylish life and Truman was in the way. More and more often, she sent him for visits to Monroeville to stay with her cousins, the Faulks.

Now, in this summer of 1930, Lillie Mae, his mother, told Jenny and Sook that Truman would be there to stay until further notice. The two "aunts" to this little boy wanted to dote on him and make his life happier.

At this moment, Nelle didn't care why he wore such fancy clothes.

"Well, what can we play, then?" she asked with her hands on her hips.

"Do you want to sit on the back steps and help me cut out pictures from magazines?" Truman asked hopefully.

Not really wanting to do something so boring, but not really wanting to hurt this eager boy's feelings, Nelle answered, "Sure."

Soon, Nelle and Truman were always together. They climbed up in the tree house and declared that it was off limits to those pesky people known as *grown-ups*. Nelle soon realized that Truman wasn't interested in the same things that most boys were. He was a master at playing jacks, where he'd bounce a small ball and while it was in the air, he'd pick up as many of the small metal stars as he could. He was quick in other ways, too. Just because he didn't like to play ball didn't mean that he was clumsy. He could turn cartwheels better than Nelle herself.

Summer days passed quickly. Every day, Nelle and Truman played together. Nelle later remembered, "If I went to a film once a month it was pretty good for me. We had to use our own devices in our play, for our entertainment. We didn't have much money. Nobody had any money. We didn't have toys, nothing was done for us, so the result was that we lived in our imaginations most of the time."

Nelle found that Truman could test her patience as a friend. Late one afternoon, they were sitting on his back steps cutting from magazines. Truman had decided they'd cut out kites.

Suddenly, for no reason, he yelled at Nelle.

"Stop that, Nelle. Keep your grimy hands off my pictures. I hate you, Nelle. I really, really do!"

Nelle never let Truman's temper tantrums bother her.

"You shut up, you silly little shrimp or I'll knock your block off," she shouted right back.

Truman Capote in his 20s (Library of Congress photo).

Once Nelle and Truman started to school, Nelle realized that other people were going to be mean to her friend.

A friend of Nelle's brother, Edwin, later remembered, "Nelle was too rough for the girls, and Truman was scared of the boys, so he just tagged on to her and she was his protector."

Other children started to call Truman "Bulldog"

because he had an under bite, so that his bottom teeth stuck out in front of his top ones just like a bulldog's do.

Margaret Murphy, a student his age, remembered Truman by the way he dressed. "He looked like a bird of paradise among a flock of crows," she said. This was not the way most boys wanted to be remembered.

So, often times, Nelle had to come to Truman's rescue at school. One of the games that some of the boys would play on the playground was called *Hot Grease in the Kitchen*. The boys stood guard around a sandpit on the playground and called out, "Hot grease in the kitchen, go round, go round!" The other children ran around the outside of this circle of boys.

Truman would do just about anything to get attention. So, he ran up and pushed into the line of boys trying to break through it into the sandpit. Of course, the boys ganged up on him, dragged him down, and started beating him.

When Nelle realized what was going on, she tore over to the crowd and yelled, "Get off of him right now!"

She pushed the bigger, older boys away and with her fists clenched dared them to touch her as she got to Truman.

He was bawling, red-faced and scratched.

"Get up, Truman and let's go inside!" Nelle commanded. She led him away from the group, looking back over her shoulder and daring them to come after her. No one dared.

When Nelle and Truman were grown-up, Nelle decided that they had come together "by a common anguish." People who heard her say this thought she must have meant because neither of them were close to their mothers. Certainly, as a little girl, Nelle was not what her mother thought a *young lady* should be and whenever his mother Lillie Mae drifted into Truman's life, she'd yell at him, "Truman, why can't you be like a normal boy your age?"

Truman later described their friendship another way. He said they were both "apart people" who were different from the other children their age.

One girl who went to school with them recalled that the other children thought Nelle and Truman were above all of them. While all of the children would be outside the Strand Theater waiting for their Saturday afternoon movie treat, Nelle and Truman huddled together and played word games instead of standing around talking like the other kids.

Those word games were just the start of the way these two friends learned the power of words.

Chapter 4

THERE WASN'T MUCH TO DO in Monroeville during the Depression. There was no public library.

The school sold books to take home, but textbooks weren't fun reading.

Most planned activities happened at the church.

Families who could afford it looked forward to Sundays. They would splurge on Sunday lunch at the Simmons Hotel for fifty-five cents. Shortly before time for the meal, a young black boy would stand on the hotel curb and ring a bell. Families would gather to feast on southern cooking—fried chicken, mashed potatoes, okra, corn, squash, cornbread, and pie for dessert.

It was a quiet life. People didn't lock their doors. Women got their housework done in the mornings so they could visit their neighbors in the afternoon and sit on the porch drinking lemonade and discussing local news and the weather.

Children were turned loose to roam around town

because no one was worried about being able to find them at the end of the day. Since parents could afford only a few toys, children made up games or things to while away the long afternoons.

Truman's father, Arch Persons, surprised Truman one Christmas with a riding toy airplane. Truman proudly demonstrated how he could pedal his shiny new toy.

Later, Truman wrote about his airplane: "It was green and had a red propeller. I was convinced that if you pedaled fast enough it would take off and fly! Now wouldn't that be something! I could just see my cousins standing on the ground while I flew about among the clouds!"

One of those cousins was Jennings Faulk Carter. Like all of the other kids in town, he and Nelle were jealous of such a fine, real toy. They came up with a grand idea.

"Nelle, we could give Truman's airplane a better take-off if we were up high somewhere," Jennings suggested.

"We couldn't get it around the branches of my tree house, though," Nelle said. "We need somewhere high and open."

The two children thought a little longer.

"Why don't we start it from the top of that old tin-roof barn behind your Cousin Jenny's house?" Nelle suggested.

Jennings thought it was a wonderful idea. There was just one problem.

"Truman wouldn't ever let us get our hands on his plane long enough to try it," Jennings said.

With a devilish smile, Nelle said, "So, Truman doesn't have to know about it."

The two children plotted and planned. They knew that Truman sometimes went away to visit his mother in New York. She had won a beauty contest with the Elizabeth Arden Company and, with a head full of dreams, moved to New York to seek fame and fortune. Nelle and Jennings had to wait for Truman to be gone on one of those visits.

Finally, that time arrived. Neither Nelle nor Jennings could keep a straight face when Truman proudly announced, "I'll be going to New York next week. I'm going to visit with my mother!"

Seeing their smug looks, he sulkily asked, "What is it? Are you glad I'm going away?"

"Of course, not, Truman," Nelle soothed. "We're just happy for you that you finally get to visit again. We know how much you miss your mama."

Truthfully, the children did know about the time that Truman drank some of the perfume that his mother had left behind in a drawer. He thought it would taste good and remind him of his mother.

Finally, the day arrived. Nelle watched Truman leave with Cousin Jenny and then ran to find Jennings.

"The coast is clear!" She shouted as soon as she saw him.

The two children ran back to the Faulks and got Truman's prized airplane from the back of the house. Giggling and plotting, they tried to act ordinary so that no one would wonder what they were doing without Truman.

When they got to the barn, they slid open the creaky door. The cool darkness of the barn blinded them for a minute as they came in from the sun. Once their eyes adjusted, they walked around the buggy, horse, and mule, looking for a ladder. They heard the Jones' hogs in the mud hole next door.

Trying to get the airplane to the roof was harder than either could imagine.

"You are going to have to push harder," Nelle yelled to Jennings who was behind her on the ladder.

"No, you've gotta pull harder, Nelle," he yelled back. "I can't do any more!"

"Do you want to give up? We can stop here and just put it back down on the..."

Before Nelle could finish, Jennings shouted, "No,

no, no. We've come this far. We can't quit now!"

Even though she was hot and sweating, Nelle had to laugh. She knew what Jennings would say before she ever asked if he wanted to quit.

Finally, they reached the roof. The sun bore down on the warm tin.

"Boy am I glad it's not the middle of summer," Nelle said. "We couldn't stand it up here."

Once they got settled on the roof, Nelle offered to let Jennings "fly" first. She said, "I'll get behind you and push to give you a running start."

Jennings took a deep breath and got ready to fly!

"Pedal, Jennings, now pedal!" Nelle shouted as she pushed the airplane down the slanted roof.

When Jennings told this story as an adult, he said:

"Everything was under control. The Trimotor Ford sailed off the edge of the barn. *I was flying!* Then all of a sudden, instead of gliding over the pigpen and fence and landing on the grassy spot, the plane started to drop. *Bloop!* Holding on for dear life, I still hadn't lost control. There were two big hogs lying in the pond. One had heard the racket of the plane rattling down the topside of the tin roof, and she raised her head out of the water just in time to see the plane ram her side with a big *Whomp!* She'd never walk straight again.

The other hog was excited, too, and as she stood

up in shock, the plane careened off the first hog and hit her head-on. I sailed out of the plane into the water, and the plane went under with the hog. Mud, trash, and manure slopped everywhere."

Nelle dashed out of the barn to pull Jennings out of the mud hole.

"Nelle, it'll never fly again," Jennings said as they looked at the plane. It was muddied, scraped up and, in their fright, the hogs stomped all over it.

"What are we going to do?" Nelle asked Jennings.

Neither of the children had an idea, but they knew they didn't want Truman to find out what they'd done. Then their problem was solved for them. Howard Faulk drove up to Jenny's house in his old pickup truck. While he was inside, the two children tied the damaged airplane to the back of the truck with a wire. When Howard drove away, the battered airplane was torn to pieces.

When Truman returned, Nelle and Jennings told him that Howard ran over his airplane and tore it up!

Later, Truman told Jennings: "I'm glad you weren't here to see me cry, big boy. I cried hard over my plane, probably more than anything in the world. I wish I was a magic person, then I'd fix it back. I'd make a lot of things right again. But then I guess there's no such thing as magic any more."

This disaster didn't ruin Nelle and Truman's friendship. In fact, they were about to get a new toy that would mean more to both of them than the airplane ever did.

View from the balcony in the old Monroe County Courthouse courtroom, where Nelle liked to visit when she was a girl (Roz Morris photo).

Chapter 5

ONE OF NELLE AND TRUMAN'S favorite pastimes was reading. Since there was no public library, they had to rely on their families to get books for them.

"When we were a bit too young to read, Brother would read many, many stories to us," Nelle later remembered.

One favorite series of books was called *The Rover Boys*. However, Nelle preferred *The Seckatary Hawkins* books. This series was based on a boys' club on the Kentucky River. The club's motto was "Fair and Square." When Nelle was old enough to read the books on her own, she wrote to the publisher asking to be a member of the club. The pledge stated: "I shall always be fair and square, possessed with strength of character, honest with God and my friends, and in later life, a good citizen." Nelle eagerly signed the pledge and became a club member.

Then, one day, Nelle and Truman received quite a surprise. A.C. called the two into the house. He cleared his throat and jangled around in his pocket. He pulled out his pocketknife, flipped it and caught it like a coin. This was a habit that everyone in Monroeville was used to seeing. A.C. cleared his throat again.

"I have something that I think the two of you may enjoy," he said. He pointed to something lying on the table.

Nelle thought, *It looks like a tired old accordion.*

Looking more closely, she gasped, "Why, it's a typewriter!"

"Yes, indeed, it is," said A.C. "Do you know how to work it?"

"I do!" piped up Truman. "You press on the letter that you want and a little bar in the back raises that letter up to that ribbon going across. When the letter hits the ribbon, that letter is printed on your paper."

"Very good, young man," said A.C. "I hope the two of you will enjoy playing with it."

However, Nelle and Truman had bigger ideas than working the typewriter. They wanted to write stories!

"Nelle, think of all we can do with this!" Truman crowed. "We can write great stories!"

"I don't know, Truman," Nelle said doubtfully. "Think of how much time it is going to take us to tap out all the words. I think we would be better off to write our stories by hand."

"Nelle," Truman pleaded. "Typing is what real writers do."

That's all it took to convince Nelle.

The tree house would have been a great place to write, but the typewriter weighed more than twenty pounds. It was too heavy to take it up and down from the tree house, so they decided to alternate "offices" between their two houses.

Once they settled down to write, they faced the problem that many writers have.

"What are we going to write about?" asked Truman that first day.

"Well, think about the boys' club in *Seckatary Hawkins*. All of the stories happen on the shore of the Kentucky River. Why couldn't Monroeville be the place where our stories happen?" Nelle suggested.

"Nelle, that is a splendid idea," Truman lisped. "We both love to people watch and there are plenty of people in Monroeville that we can tell stories about."

"We can write about Mr. Barnett down at the Barnett and Jackson Hardware store," Nelle said. "He's always willing to show us his wooden leg and tell us how he got it."

"We can write about the Monala pharmacy and how your sister, Alice, won the contest to name it,"

Truman added. "It will be fun to write about how she put together "Monroeville" and "Alabama" to make Monala. Didn't she win five dollars for doing that?"

"Yes, she did," Nelle agreed. And so the children's writing career and spying began. One of the children would say what to write very slowly while the other one clacked away on the heavy typewriter.

First, they wrote about Truman's family, the Faulks.

Jenny, her sisters Callie and Sook, and her brother Bud lived in the rambling large house. Even though they were grown up, they argued all of the time just like brothers and sisters do. Sook wasn't very bright. In fact, she acted more like a young teenager, but Nelle and Truman wrote about her sneaking a pinch of tobacco in her cheek. After she'd chew it for a bit, she'd dab away the dark, brown juice with her dainty handkerchief. There were plenty of stories to write about that.

Then, Nelle and Truman spied on a house behind theirs. In this sagging old house lived Anna Stabler.

"What a strange creature she is," Nelle whispered as they peeped through the bushes.

She and Truman stared at the woman who had a wig thrown carelessly on her head. She wore lots of red make-up and had wads of cotton stuffed in her mouth because she had no teeth.

"Nelle, is she a Negro or is she white?" Truman wanted to know.

"Nobody knows, Truman," Nelle confided. "I heard one of the grown-ups say that her mama was a Negro but when they saw I was listening, they stopped talking."

Nelle and Truman continued to stare as Anna pulled out her guitar and began to play. The children went through the bushes and sat at her feet to listen. Truman loved the music so much that he begged Jenny to buy him a guitar. Once he had learned a few chords, he would streak through the bushes to Anna's house to strum and sing with her.

Even with all of these people to write about, Nelle and Truman found one place to spy that they enjoyed more than any other. It was the old tumbledown Boulware place two doors down from the Lees. It was a dark, falling-apart house shadowed by big trees. The shutters were always closed. Children held their noses when they walked by to keep from breathing "evil vapors" that they imagined came from the house. Sometimes, they'd even cross to the other side of the street to keep from walking past the Boulware place.

Alfred E. Boulware was a businessman in town.

He and his wife Annie had three children—Mary and Sally who were in their late twenties and Alfred, Jr. who was a few years younger and called *Son*.

Mr. Boulware wouldn't do anything to keep up his house. The yard had no grass, but the dirt was swept with a straw broom. He wouldn't let anyone come on his property without his permission. The elementary school playground backed up to the Boulware's back yard. If someone hit a ball over the schoolyard fence, the children let it go for fear of being caught in Mr. Boulware's yard.

Nelle and Truman watched the house day after day with great fascination. Every day, Mary and Sally left from the broken-down house looking as neat and well dressed as anybody in town. They waved to Nelle and Truman as they passed by. Both were headed to their jobs as a dental assistant and a secretary.

"How does mean old Mr. Boulware have beautiful daughters like that?" Truman whispered one day as the girls passed by.

"But, what about Son?" Nelle smiled deliciously. "Do you really think he's tied to a bedpost in the house like everybody says?" She felt a shiver go down her spine at the thought.

The idea of a boy being tied up as a prisoner in his own home seemed like something children made up. However, most of it was true. When Son was in high school, he and two other boys got into trouble. They broke some school windows with a slingshot and broke into one of the drugstores. When they got caught, they were taken to Judge Murdock McCorvey Fountain.

"I believe that three such smart young men could benefit from a year at the state industrial school for boys," the judge ordered. *Reform school*, some called it.

The other two boys' parents agreed.

Mr. Boulware suggested something else for his son. "If you'll turn Son over to me, I can guarantee that he will never make trouble for this town again."

The judge agreed and Son was sent home with his father.

After that, Son wasn't seen by much of anyone ever again. At first, his friends from high school would crawl up to his bedroom window to try to sneak and talk to him. They passed the word that Son would be glad to do the football players' math homework for them. In return, the football players had to sneak him out of the house after midnight and take him for a ride in their cars.

After several years, all of Son's friends grew up and graduated from high school. They made lives of their own, and Son was left alone. Sometimes, neighbors saw his shadowy figure on the porch after it got dark.

During one day of spying, Nelle spotted him in the shade of a tree in the yard.

"Truman, he's not so strange!" she declared.

In 1952, Son died of tuberculosis. The marker on his grave in the First Baptist Church Cemetery says: *To Live in Hearts We Leave Behind is Not to Die.*

Nelle and Truman continued writing as often as possible. One of their stories was called "The Fire and the Flame." This writing affected both of their lives forever. Other children just didn't get it, though.

Nancie B. Robinson remembered coming over to Nelle's house to play games. "There was an old typewriter on the desk in the room, and Nelle grabbed some paper and put it in the typewriter. Truman started telling a story, and while he talked Nelle typed it. Well, they would not let me help with the story, so I just grabbed my paper dolls and went home!"

The writing business of the young authors was about to end, though. Suddenly, in the mid-1930s, Lillie Mae, Truman's mother, decided that he needed to come to New York and live with her and her new husband, Joseph Capote. From that time on, Truman came back to Monroeville only in the summers.

In 1935, Truman was adopted by his stepfather. For the rest of his life, he would be known as Truman Capote.

Nelle's Monroeville high school class picture. Her face is circled in upper right.

Chapter 6

ONCE TRUMAN GOT TO NEW YORK, his mother and stepfather enrolled him in a fancy school to prepare him for college.

Back home, Nelle continued going to school in Monroeville. Some parents in town sent their children to private school in Montgomery or Birmingham. Even though the Lees could afford to, they felt that little Nelle was too much of a free-spirit and already too unhappy with the idea of school anyway. Going away would be a lonely fate for her.

With Truman gone, Nelle drew closer to A.C. than ever. People around town wondered how A.C., who was really old enough to be Nelle's grandfather, handled such a rowdy, rough-and-tumble girl.

"Mr. Lee seemed to me to be much more of an intellectual than a physical man," recalled Joseph Blass who was A.C.'s caddie on the golf course.

Marie Faulk, one of Truman's relatives remembered, "Mr. Lee was detached, not particularly friendly, especially with children... He was not the sort of father who came up to his children, ruffled their hair, and made jokes for their amusement."

Part of the way A.C. acted had to do with the times. People like doctors and lawyers were expected to act serious and businesslike all the time. That was how people in Monroeville thought of A.C.

He was a tall man. His large, round glasses were the main feature of his face. Every weekday morning, he stepped out of the Lee home in a wrinkled three-piece suit and headed north toward his law office above the bank on the town square.

"How are you this morning, A.C.?" neighbors asked.

"Ah-hum!" A.C. cleared his throat before speaking as he was always prone to do, "I am quite fine, and you?"

A.C. listened more than he talked and often sucked on hard candy. One of his trademark gestures was to fumble with things, particularly the tiny pocket-knife that he kept in his pocket. The owner of the hardware store calmly waited when it was time for A.C. to buy a new knife. He'd choose several different pocket knives and flip each one until he found one that had the exact weight and feel that he wanted for his favorite habit.

A.C. was a busy man. Besides being a lawyer, he owned part of the town newspaper, *The Monroe Journal*, where he often wrote long editorials about taxes, drinking, unsuitable behavior, and politics. He also was a representative in the state Legislature.

One day, Nelle and Jennings spied a new sight on the school playground. The Ku Klux Klan, known for its hatred of black people and Jews, was practicing. The men saluted flags and formed up in ranks, just like army men. A.C. saw what was happening. He gathered several important Monroeville men at the courthouse. They went out and asked the Klansmen to stop their drills because it scared the children. Without any argument or disagreement, the men broke ranks.

Every Sunday, A.C. sat alone near the front of the church. His job as a deacon, or church leader, was to lead a prayer. Many times, he'd drum his pocketknife on the pew as he prayed long, burning prayers.

Because of his serious nature, most people wondered what kind of parent he was. At home, he was different from the way he was in public.

"Come on, Dody," he'd coax. "Come sit in my lap and help me read the newspaper." Other nights, he would say, "Let's solve this crossword puzzle together."

Nelle felt close to her father. They even invented a word game together.

"You know the rules," A.C. reminded Dody. "I'm thinking of a word. I'm giving you two clues. One of the clues is a letter in the word. That clue is *w*. The other clue is the number of letters in the word. That number is *five*."

Nelle, or *Dody* as she was always called at home, thought hard. "Wrong?" she asked hopefully.

"No, try again," A.C. encouraged her.

"Wrist?" Nelle tried.

"No."

"How about 'write'?" Nelle suggested.

A.C. grinned broadly. "You got it, Dody!"

Because of the game, Nelle learned many new words at a much earlier age than most children.

Whenever Nelle did things wrong, A.C. was patient with her. He didn't spank her for doing wrong; he'd just encourage her to do better. Nelle knew that she was growing up in a house where she was loved.

"Nelle just trotted at her father's heels, up and down the street," Marie Faulk Rudisill recalled.

So it was no surprise when Nelle wrote her famous book that she'd use A.C. as the model for one of her main characters, Atticus Finch. Perhaps, also, Nelle herself was Atticus' daughter, Jean Louise.

Nelle's father, A.C. Lee, left, beside photo of actor Gregory Peck who played the role of Atticus Finch in the movie To Kill a Mockingbird.

Chapter 7

THE GREAT DEPRESSION finally ended.

But, on its heels came the United State's entry into World War II. People in Monroeville joined in the war effort. A.C. helped with war bond drives to raise money. Alice volunteered for the Red Cross while Louise moved to Eufaula to wait for her husband's return from war. Edwin withdrew from Auburn University to join the Army Air Corps.

Only sixteen years old, Nelle was in her second year of high school at the beginning of the war. Like most teenagers, she was more caught up in what was happening in her own life than she was in world events.

But, there was one difference in Nelle and most teenage girls. Other girls worried about lipstick, curling their hair, and attracting the attention of the boys at Monroe County High School.

Such thoughts never entered Nelle's mind. Even though she no longer wore overalls, she didn't spend her time primping and looking good for the boys. If boys were asked what they thought of Nelle, their response would be that she was quick tempered, bold, sassy, and sure of herself.

In many pictures, Nelle held her chin high and unsmilingly faced the camera. She didn't wear lipstick, make-up or keep her hair curled. That just wasn't Nelle.

One day, Nelle strolled past the courthouse with her friends, Anne Hines and Sara Anne McCall. They stopped to watch some boys from school picking teams for a touch football game.

"A.B., I want to be put on a team," Nelle yelled out to one of the captains.

"Nelle, it's guys playing!" A.B. argued. "Why don't you girls be our cheerleaders?"

Anne and Sara Anne eagerly agreed to that idea and each of them picked a team to cheer for. But, Nelle persisted, "I don't want to cheer. I want to play!"

Anxious to get the game going, A.B. agreed to take Nelle on his team. On the first play, as the ball was snapped to A.B., he handed it off to Nelle. She took off! A player from the other team ran up to stop her. Instead of dodging him or letting the play stop by being tagged, Nelle stuck her arm straight out and knocked him down. Then, she sprinted to the goal line to score.

A.B. hollered down the field, "Nelle, we're playing touch!"

"Y'all can play that sissy game if you want to," Nelle yelled back, "but I'm playing tackle!"

Nelle didn't set out to impress people. She was who she was, and if someone didn't like that, she had no use for them.

Chapter 8

LIKE MOST OF THE TEENAGERS whose parents were fairly well off, Nelle looked forward to finishing high school and going to college. However, there were two people in Monroeville who were lifetime role models for her—and both of them were independent women.

The first one lived in Nelle's house. It was Alice, her sister, who described her job at home as "keeping the home fires burning." Since their mother Frances was too sick to tend to the younger children, Alice looked after Louise, Edwin, and Nelle until they were old enough to go off on their own.

"Alice and Nelle were as alike as a giraffe and a hippopotamus," Truman once said. They certainly didn't look or act alike. Alice was a small, thin, bird-like young lady who wore black glasses like A.C.'s. She graduated from Monroe County High School when she was sixteen and attended the Women's College of Alabama in Montgomery. After only a year in college,

Alice returned home to take care of the family. There, she started to follow in her father's footsteps—something that most people expected a son instead of a daughter to do.

Alice became a partner and associate editor of the *Monroe Journal,* her father's newspaper. She took care of the home and some of A.C.'s business while he was away working in the Alabama Legislature. Then, in 1937, when Alice was twenty-six, she moved to Birmingham to start a life of her own. She worked at the Social Security division of the Internal Revenue Service, the government office that collects taxes.

Alice enjoyed being on her own, but her independence didn't last long. She got a phone call from A.C.

"Ah-hum, Alice," he began, "Just wanted you to know that L.J. died."

Alice knew her father was talking about Mr. L.J. Bugg, one of his law partners. However, she wasn't prepared for what A.C. said next.

"I wondered if you'd think about coming back to Monroeville." A.C. paused. "That is, after you go to law school. Then you could come home to practice as the new partner in our firm."

"I have never given that a thought," Alice laughed. "Don't you think everybody would just think of me as A.C.'s little girl?"

"Honey, by the time you finish law school, you'll be over thirty," A.C. calmly replied. "I don't think anybody would think of you as a little girl!"

So, Alice enrolled in the Birmingham School of Law in 1939. She completed her studies in 1943. On a hot July afternoon, Alice went to Montgomery to take the Alabama Bar Exam, a test all lawyers must pass before they can begin working. The test took four days.

When Alice finished, she went back to her apartment in Birmingham to wait. The people in charge of the test told her she'd hear something the next day. Alice waited anxiously for her phone to ring. Finally, late in the morning, the call came. She had passed! As soon as she hung up the phone, she picked it back up to give A.C. the news.

"I passed!" Alice announced as soon as A.C. answered.

He was thrilled. "I'll get everything arranged here," he promised. "You'll be a new partner in the law office of Barnett, Bugg, and Lee before you know it!"

Only a few weeks later, Alice was back at home. Being such an independent and self-sufficient young lady, Alice soon made a name for herself as a lawyer. She became known as the "tax lady" lawyer because she learned so much about problems people had with taxes.

Nelle was seventeen years old when Alice became a Monroeville lawyer. It made a strong impression on her that a young lady could do something like this.

The other woman who had a powerful influence on Nelle was her high school English teacher, Miss Gladys Watson. Miss Watson was tall, blond and thin. She lived with her parents across the street from Nelle in a two-story yellow house with a big porch on three of its sides.

Everyone thought of Miss Watson as one of the best teachers at Monroe County High. She was also a quilter and a gardener. Nelle often saw Miss Watson outside in her yard tending to her flowers. Miss Watson didn't get married until later in her life because she liked spending her time teaching and reading.

Since Monroe County High School was so small, Miss Watson taught students English from their second year in high school, when they were sophomores, until they graduated two years later. One student remembered, "I adored her. She was very strict. She gave you two grades. One was for your grammar in a paper—and you got a whole letter taken off for any mistake, and that included commas."

Miss Watson's excellent teaching was so well

known that professors at the University of Alabama and Auburn would compliment students who wrote well by saying, "You must have taken Miss Watson."

Miss Watson loved English literature and she tried to pass on that love through her teaching. Nelle became devoted to it. She eagerly checked out any topics that Miss Watson discussed. Nelle's particular favorite was a book called *Pride and Prejudice.*

First published in 1813, *Pride and Prejudice* is a novel about life in proper country society in England. Many high school students still read it today.

This novel was written by Jane Austen—an author that Nelle later wished to be compared to.

Chapter 9

BY 1943, THE WOMEN'S COLLEGE OF ALABAMA in Montgomery was renamed Huntingdon College. Its motto was: "Enter to grow in wisdom, go forth to apply wisdom in service." Nelle wasted no time in entering this college after high school. She signed up for summer classes that began in June, just after graduating from high school in May.

The large campus was in one of Montgomery's most beautiful neighborhoods, known as Old Cloverdale, off East Fairview Avenue. As freshmen girls arrived for their first taste of college, they were greeted at Flowers Hall, the administration building. To the left and right of the building were the other important college buildings—the library, the student center, the tea room, two dormitories where the girls would live, and the infirmary, in case they were sick. On a low ridge in front of Flowers Hall was The Green, a grassy area that served as a park, playing field, and place where the May Festival was held each year.

Dr. Hubert Searcy, the college president, gave a speech to the freshmen girls the day that Nelle arrived. He said, "It may be that our greatest contribution at Huntingdon is to keep alive and strengthen those ideals for which we are fighting." He was talking about the country still being involved in World War II. He continued, "When we see the tragedy of the world at war, we see the need for greater understanding among men...and acquaintance with music, literature, and art, and a deeper knowledge of the relations of people."

Huntingdon's goal was to educate young women with just those sorts of things. The college also insisted on religious education for their students, so every morning Chapel was at 8 a.m. and girls weren't allowed to miss the service unless they could prove they'd been in church somewhere else at the time.

The college provided chances for the young women to improve their social graces as well. Every night, the girls ate at tables for eight. At the head of each table was one of their female teachers. The food was passed around the table and each girl had to take at least a small amount of each dish that was offered. Tables were set so that the girls learned which piece of silverware to use for each part of the meal. One of the jobs of the teacher at the table was to peek under the tablecloth during the meal to be sure that none of the girls had their legs crossed. Each girl was expected to sit with her feet flat on the floor with her knees tightly together. Once each month, the girls were expected to dress in evening dresses for dinner.

If the girls decided to go into the city of Montgomery, they were expected to wear hats, gloves, dresses, and high-heel shoes. Even when they were on campus and going to class, girls had to wear dresses or skirts and blouses. The only time girls could wear whatever they wanted was when they were in their dormitories.

From the day Nelle arrived at Huntingdon, she didn't fit in with the other girls in her dorm, Massey Hall. Other girls wore pressed slacks and matching blouses when they were relaxing in the dorm. Not Nelle. She wore jeans or white Bermuda shorts. Other girls wore makeup. Not Nelle. She brushed her hair only once a day, never curled it, and thought that a clean face was all she needed. She skipped the monthly formal dinner so she wouldn't have to wear an evening dress.

At this time, people didn't know that smoking was a health hazard. Women thought it made them look stylish to light up a cigarette. Nelle didn't even do this like the other girls. More than one girl was shocked as she passed Nelle's bedroom door and glanced inside.

There was Nelle, feet propped on her desk, dressed in blue jeans and a wrinkled shirt, puffing away on a pipe!

Worst of all, the girls soon realized that Nelle often used bad words when she talked.

One girl remembered Nelle in college and said, "I never heard any of my friends use four-letter words. No one in my family did."

At the end of the first quarter of school, the two girls who lived in the dorm room with Nelle asked her to find new roommates. They didn't want her to room with them. Nelle didn't seem to mind, and went on with her studies. She made the honor roll. Other people on campus realized what a good athlete she was and often picked her first in volleyball and soccer games. She made friends with other people on campus, too. People realized she was very kind and sensitive to others.

It was February 12, 1945, the date for one of the formal dinners on campus to honor Valentine's Day. Girls dashed from room to room borrowing jewelry, hair bows, and other things to dress up for the special dinner. Of course, Nelle didn't plan to eat at all because she wasn't going to dress up in a formal. She'd rather go hungry!

The weather grew stormy. Wind slashed at the windows, tree branches snapped, and lightning lit the sky. The lights went out in Massey Hall. The formal was cancelled as girls took cover. The girls were fearful as the horrible storm continued outside and the lights stayed off. Finally, at bedtime, the lights flickered back on. The storm that spawned a tornado had ended, but not before it killed 26 people and destroyed more than a hundred Montgomery homes.

Nelle was resting comfortably in her room when Mary Nell Atherton passed by. Mary Nell looked worried.

"Are you all right?" Nelle asked.

"I'm fine," Mary Nell assured her, "but my roommate isn't. She is terrified! She keeps looking out the window, afraid that the storm is coming back."

The girl continued to worry days after the tornado was gone. She was terrified that another tornado would come. She couldn't sleep. All of her friends were worried about her.

"One afternoon," Mary Nell remembered," Nelle came down to the room because she'd heard my roommate was so afraid she couldn't sleep."

"I'd be glad to stay up with you and keep you company," Nelle offered, "because I can't sleep, either."

Even though Nelle was different than most of the other girls, she was concerned and caring of others.

By the end of her freshman year, Nelle decided she would transfer to the University of Alabama in Tuscaloosa. She had not fit in at Huntingdon and she knew it. After the first roommates asked her to move out, Nelle spent most of her free time in her new room alone or in the library silently studying. She was ready to start over.

As the final semester ended, Nelle could hardly wait to get home. One day, she saw A.B. Blass, her old football friend from Monroeville, drive up in his car. He had come to get his fiancée, the girl he planned to marry. When Nelle saw him, she ran up to his car and said, "A.B., you going back to Monroeville? Hold on, and let me get my things!"

"But, Nelle…" A.B. started to protest. Nelle didn't stop to listen. She ran to the dorm to gather her things. In just a few minutes, she was back and climbed into the back seat behind A.B. and his girlfriend.

A.B. tried to make Nelle understand, "Nelle, I haven't seen my girlfriend in a long time."

"We can talk about that later, A.B.," Nelle said. "Right now, let's just get going!"

"But, Nelle…" A.B. tried again.

"Are you going to Monroeville or aren't you?"

Nelle demanded.

"Nelle, we might not go straight home," A.B. admitted. "I want some time with my girl by myself."

"Suit yourself!" Nelle shouted as she got out of the car and slammed the door.

In looking back at the time they were at Huntingdon, Catherine Helms remembered Nelle. "That was an era when you did the proper thing," she said. "And your mother was horrified if you didn't. That was never part of Nelle's persona—she didn't care! It must have taken a colossal amount of courage to be different!"

Perhaps when she got to the University of Alabama, Nelle would find a way to fit in even if she was different.

Chapter 10

THE UNIVERSITY OF ALABAMA was nicknamed "The Country Club of the South" in the 1940s. Young men returning from the war were eager to pick up where they'd left off. They wanted to date girls and get an education. The girls at the University were thrilled to have boys back on campus. During the war years, the University looked almost like a girls' school.

"We gave boys' names to some of the girls so that we could hear the sound of the name," one girl remembered.

One of the highlights of this return to a simpler Southern lifestyle was the students' interest in the Panhellenic clubs—fraternities for boys and sororities for girls. Getting into a sorority at Alabama was no easy feat. Before classes began each fall, young ladies turned out to put their best foot forward at the fifteen houses that dotted Sorority Row. Special events such as ice water teas, receptions, and parties were scheduled so that the sorority girls could look over the new girls who wanted to join and pick only the best of the best to be a part of their sorority.

Chi Omega was one of the sororities on campus. The campus yearbook, *Corolla,* stated that the Chi O house was one that "specialized in blondes—long, short, thin, and broad."

Many sorority girls proudly wore fraternity pins, showing that they were promised to a young man in a fraternity.

This setting didn't seem like a place for Nelle. However, eager to start fresh at a new college, she put her name on the list of girls to go through Rush Week and all of its activities during the fall of 1945. Each day, eager girls dressed their best and visited the sorority houses to be checked out to see if they fit.

Nelle liked the humor she found behind these doors. Sorority girls greeted their rushees—as the hopeful new girls were called—with songs about fraternities and drinking. Nelle already had one friend in Chi O, Sylvia Parnell, who had grown up in Monroeville. Sylvia was classy and looked on by other sorority girls with awe.

After the first visit to Chi Omega, Nelle liked what she saw. She eagerly scanned the list of girls who would be invited back to be further examined. To her delight and surprise, her name was on the Chi O list!

Her surprise grew when she was invited to join this group.

However, just as many people learn as they grow up, Nelle could not change who she really was, nor did she want to. She still chain-smoked cigarettes and didn't want to dress up. On Friday nights while other Chi O girls bustled around getting ready for dates and dances with their fraternity boyfriends, Nelle tromped through the living room of the Chi O house dressed in jeans and a sweatshirt, eagerly looking forward to eighteen holes of golf after a week of studying.

It wasn't long before other people noticed Nelle, and not in the way she'd hoped.

"She had long flat shoes, long straight hair, a slight slump, probably because she carried a black portable typewriter in one hand and a stack of books and papers in the other," remembered Barbara Moore, one of the girls who made fun of Nelle. "I never saw her with anyone and wondered if she were lonely."

Barbara belonged to Phi Mu, another campus sorority, and she further admitted, "I'm ashamed to admit that we made fun of her. Never around her, but behind her back. Today she would be called a campus nerd."

Another girl described Nelle. "She was a little mannish-looking. When girls had long hair and did things with it, her hair was short."

Mary Anne Berryman recalled Nelle as "A little bit thick in the middle. Nothing very stylish." Yet, she did have something nice to add. "She had beautiful large, dark brown eyes that were quite piercing."

Yet once again in her life, Nelle had trouble fitting in. Nelle knew she wasn't a frilly, dress-up kind of girl and was comfortable with herself. She tells a story about one night at the sorority house when the girls thought a burglar was inside.

"People poured into the lounge with angry expressions on their faces. Then, Lila said the word 'burglar.' From nowhere appeared the most complete collection of blunt instruments I have ever seen: coke bottles, tennis racquets, pokers, hair dryers, and even a pair of ice tongs. But, nobody would go downstairs."

Nelle tells how the girls decided to call the police. When the police came, the girls shouted down to them that a burglar might be inside and they needed to search the house.

"I was chosen to escort them through the premises," Nelle said, "and when we got up to the attic the watchman gave me his flashlight and said, 'You go first.'"

Even as Nelle could laugh about being different, she still wanted a place to fit in. She found that place at the Alabama Union building during her first fall on campus. Nelle climbed the flight of stone stairs all the while staring up at the third floor. On this floor were the offices of the university's student publications. On one side, student writers eagerly turned out the *Crimson White,* the campus newspaper. Nelle deliberately strode up to Bill Mayes, one of the editors.

"I'd like to offer my services to the newspaper," she said. "I could work as a stringer covering events and meetings on campus."

"I really appreciate the offer," Bill responded. "But, most of our news stories go to people who are majoring in journalism, and they already have lots of experience."

Disappointed but determined, Nelle made her way to the other side of the room. Here were the writers and editors for the *Rammer Jammer,* the campus humor magazine. Nelle found her place! She wrote funny stories about the upcoming homecoming events on campus. Also, she knew that the more stories she got published in *Rammer Jammer,* the better her chances for being accepted as an experienced writer and writing for the campus newspaper.

Nelle waited patiently until summer 1946. Many students don't go to classes in the summer. They go home, get jobs, and rest before the next year of classes begin. Not Nelle. She stayed on campus to take a few courses. Her main purpose, though, was to write for the *Crimson White*. She knew that many of the paper's current writers would be going home.

Nelle was ready. She went back to Bill Mayes, who was in charge of the paper for the summer.

"Bill, what if I write an at-large column during the summer?" Nelle suggested.

"What do you mean?" Bill asked.

"You know, something that comments on the passing scene here on campus—something to lighten up the editorials?" Nelle explained.

Bill liked the idea.

So began Nelle's *career* as a writer for the campus paper. She called her column "Caustic Comment" and spent long hours creating stories filled with great description and funny jokes about campus and world events. She made fun of advertisements on the radio, student activities on campus, and other things. One trait of Nelle's that spilled into her writing was her use of curse words. At that time, students on campus weren't used to seeing such words in print.

One student remembered, "'Caustic Comment' is the best reading there is—but so much more fun if not slapped on like red paint on an old barn."

Even after that summer of writing for the campus

paper, Nelle realized that her talents were better suited for the *Rammer Jammer.* Still sending articles to the campus paper, Nelle was appointed editor-in-chief of the humor magazine. Other people realized this was a better fit for Nelle, too.

"She dressed differently, ate differently, talked differently than most. She thought differently, too," said John Hamner, later to become an Alabama newspaperman, "and those differences made her stand out."

By the fall of her junior year, Nelle was firmly

Photos of Nelle in the 1947 University of Alabama yearbook, The Corolla.

settled into her magazine job. She was ready to take on a new adventure. Nelle enrolled in law school! At that time, students who kept a C average their first two years of college could apply to start law school studies.

Nelle turned in a humor piece to the campus paper about her experience signing up for law school. Titled "What Price Registration?" Nelle cleverly wrote about her experience.

"There, upon the steps (forty-six of them) sat men, men, men! In some confusion I began climbing those steps, amid the usual medley of whistles (I haven't figured that deal out yet; I'm as ugly as sin)."

Nelle goes on to describe her ordeal with getting all the correct paperwork turned in on time. She became a law school student and continued as editor for the magazine. She was a busy girl! She was even featured in a front page article in the *Crimson White:*

Wild about football, she played center on the fourth grade team in Monroeville, her hometown. Her favorite person is her sister "Bear"...Lawyer Lee will spend her future in Monroeville. As for literary aspirations she says, "I shall probably write a book some day. They all do."

Nelle already had a different idea about her future. When classes ended in May, she took the train to

Evergreen, headed for home. Usually, she stayed on campus all summer, but this one was different. Nelle looked forward to her brother's wedding in June. Edwin was marrying Sara Anne McCall, Nelle's childhood friend and classmate. Even though it meant really dressing up, Nelle was excited about being a bridesmaid in the wedding.

As the train rumbled along the tracks, Nelle's excitement was clouded by a sense of dread. She had already talked to A.C. once about her ideas, and she knew it was time to talk to him again.

Nelle's thoughts raced furiously. *I don't like law school. No, in fact, I hate studying law. I know how much A.C. wants another lawyer in the family. He just doesn't understand.*

Nelle's family eagerly greeted her when she got home. There was so much to do to get ready for the wedding. Nelle decided that she couldn't put off talking to A.C. again, though.

"A.C., once all of this wedding business is over, I want us to talk again," Nelle began.

"Ah-hum, what is it you need, Dody?" A.C. asked absently.

"It's not something I need," Nelle stated bluntly. "It's actually something I don't need. I don't want to go back to law school. I want to be a writer."

Normally calm and encouraging to everything that Nelle had to say, A.C.'s face turned red. "Now, Dody, just because Truman thinks he is working on his first great novel, it doesn't mean a thing. There's not a bit of money to be made in writing like that. If you want to be a writer, finish up law school first so you'll have something to fall back on. Then, if you still want to write, you can take over running our newspaper here at home."

A.C. warmed to his own idea. "I'm almost seventy years old, Dody. I'd love to have more time to play golf and less time to work. I'd love to take it easy. If you don't want to practice law, you could do our family a big service by taking over *The Monroe Journal.* Alice is so busy with our law practice and even though Edwin and Sara Anne are going to be here, you know his job is in engineering. You don't have to practice law at Barnett, Bugg, & Lee. But at least, finish your degree in case you change your mind."

Nelle just nodded. There was no sense in arguing right then.

The wedding was on June 28, 1947 in Monroeville. As is normal for summer in the South, the weather was steamy. The wedding was scheduled for six o'clock at First Methodist Church with hopes that some of the day's heat would pass. The reception was outside at Sara Anne's home. Nelle enjoyed the partying after the wedding, but her heart was heavy. She didn't know what she was going to do.

The rest of the summer passed quickly with Edwin and Sara Anne settling into life in Monroeville. Alice announced that she was staying permanently at home, too.

"This is where I need to be now," Alice said unselfishly. "With Mother having to be in the hospital in Selma so much, yet once again, I need to keep the home fires burning."

So, in August, Nelle boarded the train in Evergreen. She headed back to Tuscaloosa, determined to give law school one more try.

Chapter 11

AS THE TRAIN RUMBLED ALONG, taking Nelle back to Tuscaloosa, her troubled thoughts came back. There were about one hundred students enrolled in law school at the University. Only about a dozen were women. The classes were hard and the students were ready for action. Many of the men in her class had been soldiers. They were eager to do well in law school and get into practice as soon as possible. The women worked hard to prove themselves just as worthy. As always, Nelle thought she didn't fit in. It wasn't what she wanted to do.

One student from Nelle's criminal law class remembered that she "would not have been noticed except for the fact that she was in a large class of males." Then, using words that would often be used to describe Nelle later in life she added, "To say that she was reclusive is an understatement. She was very quiet; spoke to no one—except when the instructor called on her to respond. Even then, she did so with as few words as possible."

Even though her heart wasn't in it, Nelle worked hard in her classes. She attended study groups, trying to learn about rulings that applied to cases her class studied. At the time Nelle was in law school, there was a special bonus for students who passed their exams in every subject. They wouldn't be required to take the Alabama Bar Exam when they graduated. Because of this, though, the instructors in the law school classes made their exams as hard as possible.

Nelle didn't want to disappoint A.C. Often she thought that if she'd just gone after a four-year degree instead of law school, she'd be finished with school by the end of the year. However, law school meant she had another year to go.

Nelle thought, *A.C. sold the newspaper because he knew I wasn't going to come back and take that over for him. I can't hurt him anymore. I'm terrified that I can't pass those horrible exams, but not because I'm not smart enough—It's just that I don't care about it! I wish I was more like "Bear" and loved all of this law stuff, but I don't.*

Surprisingly, back home, A.C. realized how unhappy Nelle was. He knew she didn't love studying law the way Alice had. Maybe he could offer her something new. Maybe it would show her that by choosing a law career she would make enough money to travel and write as a sideline. Nelle jumped at A.C.'s offer.

On April 29, 1948, the *Monroe Journal* announced, *Miss Nelle Lee, University of Alabama law student and daughter of Mr. and Mrs. A.C. Lee of Monroeville, has been accepted as an exchange student at Oxford University in England during the coming summer. She will sail from New York on June 16.*

Nelle could hardly wait! She was actually going to visit the places that she'd dreamed of as she read her beloved books by Jane Austen. She thought about Miss Watson, her high school English teacher, and how she'd encourage Nelle's love of English literature. Oh, the places she'd finally get to see!

Nelle dogged through her spring classes, counting the days until she could go home and get ready for the grand adventure. Student exchange programs with countries overseas were a new idea after World War II. Nelle would be part of the program's second summer. The only way to get her to England was aboard a troop ship that had been used to take soldiers to and from Europe. To her, it was as grand as a cruise ship!

On the morning of June 16, Nelle was in New York ready to board the *Marine Jumper,* a drab olive-gray ship. It was huge— one of the largest built during the war. It was one and a half times longer than a football field and 71-feet wide. The only thing that had been done to dress up the ship was a band of red, white, and blue painted on the front of it. Students slept in double bunks. One shower served 35 people. Meals were fattening and greasy.

But, the ship set sail and so did Nelle's dreams.

On Friday, June 25, Nelle heard the call she'd been waiting for. The ship was landing in Plymouth, England. She quickly ate breakfast and waited impatiently for the motor launch to pull alongside and take her to her dream. Once she got on land, she was startled by all that was going on. The English that she was hearing spoken was nothing like the slow, syrup-like southern drawl to which she was accustomed. At times, she even had trouble understanding what was being said. Then, she was led to customs and given directions on how to collect her luggage. Nelle was expected to listen to a clerk explain all about British money—pounds, crowns, shillings, and so on. Nelle was so confused. Finally, when it was time for her to buy a ticket for a train ride to Oxford, she held out her hand filled with money to the clerk and said, "Take what you need."

For four hours, Nelle soaked in the English countryside. Finally, the train crossed the Isis River on the western side of Oxford University. Nelle saw Christ Church and the famous Tom Tower whose bell had rung since the late 1600s. A feeling of peace overcame the often out-of-place girl.

The summer was fabulous. Nelle enrolled in a class on twentieth-century literature, but she was allowed to attend any other lectures that she wanted. And she did! One day, she went to the Bodleian Library where she strolled along rows of books that were hundreds of years old. This was who she really was and this was what she wanted.

Nelle hated for the summer to end. She walked along the very streets that Jane Austen had walked. She lived each day filled with books.

When Nelle returned home, Alice remarked that "She fell in love with England."

However, it was time to go back to her final year of law school. Nelle made it through the fall semester often daydreaming about her trip to England. Also, it didn't help that Truman had published his first novel, *Other Voices, Other Rooms,* last year and was getting rave reviews.

I know I can't have success like Truman's on my first try, Nelle thought, *but I've just got to give it a try. There is no point in my staying in law school anymore.*

Heck, I'll probably fail the exams anyway!

So, during the Christmas holidays, Nelle approached A.C. once again.

"A.C., I've decided I'm going to drop out of law school," Nelle stated firmly.

"Nelle, that's foolish," A.C. replied. "If you leave now, you won't have a degree at all—not even a bachelor's degree in any subject. Your years of college will be wasted! What do you think you could possibly be trained to do without a degree?"

Nelle's answer shocked and angered A.C.

"I plan to go to New York, find a job, and," she said after a long pause, "I plan to write!"

"Uh-hum," A.C. familiarly began. "I've tried to support you in everything you've ever done, Dody. You know that. I am more than ready to pay for you to finish law school. I've always planned for that. But, I will not pay for a pack of daydreams—for you to run off to New York without any idea of how you'll live or survive."

"A.C., you know me," Nelle concluded. "When I've made up my mind to do something, I find a way. I've made up my mind, and I will find a way.

Nelle withdrew from the University Of Alabama School Of Law at the end of the first semester of her senior year. She never looked back.

Chapter 12

AFTER MAKING HER GREAT DECISION, Nelle left the University and went home to Monroeville. She planned to live there for a few months and save money. Nelle knew that living in New York was expensive and she'd have to find a job just as soon as she got there.

A.C. worried about Nelle's plan, but they didn't talk about it much. He knew that once Dody had her mind made up, she would stick to it. A.C. didn't want Nelle's heart to be broken. He thought this was just a wild scheme she had made up, and he certainly didn't think that there was any way that two well-known writers would come from the tiny town of Monroeville. By this time, Truman was a great literary success.

I like Truman just fine, A.C. thought to himself. *I guess I helped him get started on this writing thing with the typewriter as well as that pocket dictionary that I gave him one time. Why, he carried that thing around until it fell apart. I'm proud of what Truman has done for himself especially after his hard childhood. But, I don't want Dody to get stars in her eyes over what Truman has done. What grand ideas she has. She thinks she's going to go off to New York and write a book and get it published just like that. I guess I'll have to start thinking about how I can help her when she comes back home all disappointed...*

A.C.'s thoughts were interrupted by Nelle.

"I know you hate to hear this, A.C.," Nelle said, "But it is time to go."

Nelle's bags were packed and waiting. The two of them climbed into the car and A.C. turned south, away from the courthouse square. Nelle took one last look back as the clock at the top of the courthouse disappeared from view. A.C. steered the car toward Evergreen, where he'd taken Nelle may times before to catch the train to Tuscaloosa. Both of them knew this time was different, very different.

Nelle looked out the passenger window and tried to memorize every detail about her little town. She thought about children running in the yard, holding a Duke's mayonnaise jar, and catching lightning bugs on a summer night. She thought about how news spread from neighbor to neighbor by evening visits rocking on front porches to escape the day's heat. If a person didn't get their fill of daily news that way, there were always the telephone party lines where you could pick up your phone and hear conversations from at least ten other neighbors who were on the same line as you.

Caught up in her own thoughts, Nelle was startled to see that they were already in Evergreen. The Louisville and Nashville Railroad train stood in front of her. Saying good-bye to A.C. was hard.

"I'll be fine, A.C.," Nelle said. "You know I will. I am good at taking care of myself."

"Ah-hum," A.C.'s throat clearing habit was more choked than usual. "Just remember that there's nothing wrong with admitting you've made a mistake, Dody. You can always come back home."

"Don't worry, I won't have to," Nelle assured him with more confidence than she actually felt. "You'll see, I'm going to write and get a book published! Now, you go on back and take care of everything at home and don't worry about me. Lord knows, you've got enough to worry about!"

Nelle found a cold-water flat, which was one small room crowded with furniture and a small bed. The apartment wasn't far from where Truman had rented his first apartment when he came to New York. Also, it wasn't far from Central Park, a New York landmark. Nelle's old neighborhood housed many immigrants—people who had come to America from other countries. These new Americans loved to talk about the success of one of their local boys, Lou Gehrig, a famous baseball player for the New York Yankees.

Truman tried to help Nelle get settled in New York. He tried to get her a job as a writer, but nothing happened there. So, Nelle got a job in a bookstore.

Maybe I can meet some writers here, Nelle thought doubtfully as she unpacked books and put them on shelves.

It didn't take Nelle long to realize that New York was quite expensive. When she paid her rent from her paycheck, she only had about twenty-five dollars left for food. Her apartment only had a hot-plate—one burner—to heat food, so she used her money to buy soups and stew. But no matter how hard things got, Nelle was determined not to let A.C. know.

Finally, in 1950, Nelle found a different job. She worked at Eastern Airlines as a ticket agent. After learning the job, she was transferred to British Overseas Air Corporation (BOAC). The work wasn't glamorous, but Nelle imagined great adventures for herself if she could afford the discount tickets to England that the company offered employees. Even though she made more money with the airline, Nelle still didn't have extra money to use for airplane tickets.

Every night, Nelle sat down in her apartment to write. She used a door that had been taken down from its hinges as her desk. It was hard to concentrate with all of the outside hustle and bustle. Besides, after working all day, Nelle was tired.

She looked at her collection of books, her sharpened pencils, and her writing materials.

Now what am I going to write about? Nelle wondered.

Then, she remembered the advice she'd been given many times about writing.

Write about what you know.

She could do that. Nelle could write all about her small town of Monroeville. After all, she'd been spying on its people and writing about them since she was a little girl. Her thoughts started to grow.

Nelle worked and wrote and visited Monroeville when she had a chance. Then, on June 2, 1951, Frances Lee died. Even though her death had been expected, Nelle was only 25 years old, very young to lose her mother. After trying to get over that blow, Nelle was devastated six weeks later. Her beloved brother, Edwin, had been discovered dead in his bed at Maxwell Air Force base where he had been recalled into duty. Earlier in the day, Edwin played in a softball game at the base, yet no one could explain what caused him to have a brain hemorrhage, or bleeding, that killed him.

After Edwin's funeral that July, Nelle planned to return to New York and her writing career. That meant Alice, or "Bear," would be stuck with "keeping the home fires burning." A.C. was getting old. Louise lived in Eufaula. And Nelle was off to New York to work in a low paying job while she wrote stories.

Alice explained her situation to people by saying, "Nelle's got an itch to go to New York and write."

Nelle continued working all day and writing at night whenever she had the chance. In the fall of 1954, Truman invited her to go with him to rehearsals of a Broadway musical. Truman helped to write the show's book and words for the songs. He thought Nelle would enjoy seeing backstage of a Broadway theater.

At first, Nelle didn't want to go. She needed to spend her free time writing. But this might be a pleasant break after all. Little did Nelle realize what a break it would be. At the theater that day, Nelle met Michael Martin Brown. He was about Edwin's age, had started his career as a teacher, and now lived successfully by creating and writing words for songs. Nelle adored Michael's sense of humor. After a fun conversation, Nelle and Michael discovered that they only lived about ten minutes from each other, if they took the subway. Michael invited Nelle over to meet his wife.

Nelle recalled her first glimpse of Joy Brown. Expecting a young mother chasing two children around, Nelle was amazed by this "ethereal, utterly feminine creature." Just as Nelle and Michael hit it off as instant friends, so did she and Joy. Nelle visited them often. The three friends gathered around the piano and sang show songs. Sometimes, Michael and Joy convinced Nelle to read some of her stories. She was embarrassed, but thrilled that they liked what she wrote.

Nelle planned to go home for Christmas in 1956. She loved a visit south to refresh her spirits from the harsh, cold winters that she hated in New York. Nelle imagined getting home, loaded with gifts, to be welcomed by Alice and A.C. She knew they'd drive over and visit Louise and her family while she was home. Nelle realized she was homesick and could hardly wait for her Christmas vacation to begin.

Then, she got word that she could only take off on Christmas Eve and Christmas Day. The airline was swamped with people wanting to fly. Nelle was crushed! There was no way she could go home to Monroeville. That evening she wrote:

New York streets shine wet with the same gentle farmer's rain that soaks Alabama's winter fields...I missed Christmas away from home, I thought.

As soon as Michael and Joy Brown heard that Nelle was stuck in the city for the holiday, they invited her to share Christmas with them.

"Why don't you pack a bag and stay overnight?" Joy offered. "We'll get you off for work the morning after Christmas."

Lonesome and homesick, Nelle agreed. Normally, if she had a day off from work, Nelle slept late, but on this Christmas morning, Michael and Joy's children plowed into her room and demanded that she get up so everyone could open gifts.

Michael had built a roaring fire and everyone quickly gathered around the tree to exchange gifts. During the two years that Nelle had known her new friends, they'd never given each other expensive gifts because the Browns knew that Nelle had little money to spare. This year, Nelle was proud of a portrait of the founder of the *Edinburgh Review* that she'd found for Michael for 35 cents. Also, she'd gotten Joy a complete set of books by Lady Margot Asquith at a used book store.

Nelle proudly handed out her gifts. Suddenly, she felt shocked and disappointed. There were no more gifts under the tree. Maybe Michael and Joy thought that inviting her to their family Christmas was their gift.

Ashamed of herself for being selfish, Nelle tried to look happy.

"We haven't forgotten you, Nelle," Joy finally laughed. "Look on the tree."

A white envelope stood out against the Christmas tree's green branches. It was labeled, "Nelle."

"Open it! Open it!" the children encouraged.

Nelle opened the envelope and read, "You have one year off from your job to write whatever you please. Merry Christmas."

Nelle looked up, puzzled. "What does this mean?" she asked her friends.

"Just what it says," Michael replied. "We're paying for you to take a year off from work and write."

"That's a huge gamble for you both," Nelle cautioned. "It's too great a risk."

"It's not a risk. It's a sure thing," Michael replied confidently.

Later Nelle wrote that her friends had given her "a full, fair chance for a new life."

She was amazed by their kindness, but there was something more.

"*Our faith in you* was really all I had heard them say," Nelle wrote.

She was determined not to let them down.

Chapter 13

NELLE COULDN'T BELIEVE her good fortune. *Concentrate on writing!* She told herself sternly. She wrote to a friend: "I have a horrible feeling that this will be the making of me, that it will be goodbye to the joys of messing about. So, for the coming year I have laid in 3 pairs of Bermuda shorts, since I shall rarely emerge from 1539 York Avenue."

Nelle knew she'd have to watch her money carefully. The Brown's Christmas gift would pay her bills and feed her if she watched each penny. Now, she had no excuse, but to get to work. Nelle set up her routine. She got up late each morning, drank coffee and then went to work—all day long. Sometimes she wrote until midnight. She decided that all she needed was "paper, pen, and privacy."

Michael and Joy continued to help Nelle. Michael insisted that she take a few of her short stories to an agent, and he sent her to Annie Laurie Williams.

"I walked around the block three times before I

could muster the courage to go in and give the stories to the agent," Nelle said. "At the time, I was very shy. Finally, I rushed in, left the manuscripts with the secretary, and left. I prayed for a quick death and forgot about it."

It turned out that Annie Laurie Williams was the wrong person for Nelle to see. Annie Laurie helped to turn books into movies. But, she met with Nelle and explained what she could do.

"My husband, Maurice Crain, works with book publications," Annie Laurie explained. Annie Laurie Williams kept her unmarried name at work, so she wasn't called Mrs. Crain. "I'll get him to read your work."

Ten days later, Nelle got a phone call. Maurice Crain wanted to meet with her. Nelle met him in a New York restaurant. The short, powerful-looking man didn't look like a book agent to her. However, he jumped right to business.

Writers often have a hard time hearing criticism about their work. Nelle sat quietly as Maurice tore apart her stories. Finally, he said, "I think 'Snow on the Mountain' is the only one that I might be able to place."

Nelle was grateful for that much.

Then, Mr. Crane dashed her hopes again. "Short

stories are hard to sell. Have you thought about writing a novel?"

Nelle had thought about it, but when she was with the airline and writing in her spare time, writing a novel just seemed like too big a task. Now, she had no excuse.

She returned to Crain's office in January 1957 with another short story as well as the first fifty pages of a novel that she called *Go Set a Watchman.* A week later, she brought him another hundred pages. From that day on, she continued to bring more of the book each week. By May, she and Crain made many changes and corrections. He had one final thought before he was ready to send it to a publisher.

"I don't like the title," he told Nelle bluntly. "It sounds like the book has to do with clocks or something."

"Do you have any other ideas?" Nelle asked meekly.

"Why don't you name it after your main character?" Crain suggested.

Nelle's main character was a man modeled after her own father, A.C. She had gotten the name for her character from the writings of a famous Roman from long ago. His name was Cicero and he was known as a Roman statesman, lawyer, and philosopher. Many of

Cicero's ideas were explained through his letters to his friend, Atticus. So, Nelle chose Atticus as the name of her main character, a country lawyer from South Alabama.

The book would be called *Atticus*.

With this matter settled, Maurice Crain sent the first version of Nelle's novel to the offices of J.B. Lippincott, a New York publishing company.

"Now, we just have to wait," he explained to Nelle.

Not wanting to waste any of the precious gift of time that she had, Nelle went straight back to work. By the end of May, she returned to Mr. Crain's office with 111 pages of a second novel that she called *The Long Goodbye*. Mr. Crain was delighted that Nelle didn't waste her time.

A few days later, Nelle received a phone call. It was Mr. Crain.

"Lippincott wants to meet with you about *Atticus,*" he said.

Nelle's pen froze. Was she really ready for this?

Nelle timidly entered the Lippincott offices. All of the editors in the room were men except for one. Nelle's attention was drawn to a middle-aged woman with iron gray hair pulled into a tight bun. Dressed in a business suit, the editor introduced herself, "My name is Theresa von Hohoff—but, I prefer to be called 'Tay'."

The entire meeting was terrifying to Nelle. The editors talked on and on about *Atticus*.

"The characters stood on their own two feet, they were three-dimensional," one editor complimented.

Another editor said, "But, the whole thing is more a series of short stories than a full novel."

As the editors continued to suggest ways for Nelle to improve her book, she nodded and politely answered, "Yes, sir."

Finally, the meeting drew to an end. The editors wished her well and hoped to see her again—after she'd made changes.

Tay Hohoff hoped Nelle wasn't too discouraged.

"Her draft of a novel was clearly not the work of an amateur," Hohoff said. "In fact, it was hard to believe that Nelle was in her early thirties and had waited until now to approach a publisher."

Tay Hohoff agreed to work with Nelle as her editor. As Ms. Hohoff got to know Nelle better, she realized, "What Nelle wanted with all of her being was to *write*—not merely to 'be a writer.'"

By the end of the summer, Nelle turned in another edited copy of her book.

"It is better. It isn't *right,* though," Ms. Hohoff told Nelle.

The two women continued to work on Nelle's novel.

"I found that editors' teeth were made more for talking than biting," Nelle recalled. "and, that we could be friends."

Ms. Hohoff thought that Nelle's willingness to rewrite and change things in her novel would help get the book ready for publishing.

Later, Nelle would say that she was more of a "rewriter' than a writer.

"She spent her days and nights in the most intense efforts to set down what I wanted to say in the way which would best say it to the reader," Ms. Hohoff said.

Realizing Nelle's efforts, Ms. Hohoff even got Lippincott to offer Nelle a contract with a few thousand dollars in advance money to keep her going. It was a good thing that the money came in.

Nelle continued making changes and corrections. Ms. Hohoff continued asking for more.

"We talked it out, sometimes for hours," Ms. Hohoff remembered. "And sometimes she came around to my way of thinking, sometimes I to hers, sometimes the discussion would open up an entirely new line of country."

One of their discussions rolled around to Nelle's pen name, or the way she would sign herself as the author. Nelle hated when people mispronounced her name and called her "Nellie" by mistake. Being an author from the South, she worried that people would assume "Nellie," a very southern name, was her own. Instead, she wanted to use her middle name as her byline. She wanted it to be written by "Harper Lee." Ms. Hohoff agreed.

One night, Nelle was sitting at her makeshift door desk rereading a page in her typewriter. She read it over and over. Suddenly, in disgust, she grabbed up everything she'd written that day, walked over to the window, and threw it out into the snow.

She called Ms. Hohoff. "I can't do this!" she moaned. "I just threw everything I'd written today out into the snow."

"March outside right now and get it!" Ms. Hohoff commanded.

Tired and discouraged, Nelle trounced out in the cold and collected her writing.

"I knew I could never be happy being anything but a writer…I kept at it because I knew it had to be my first novel, for better or for worse."

In the spring of 1959, Nelle reached out to one of her former role models. She asked her former English teacher, Miss Watson, who was now Mrs. Burkett, if she'd read it and make corrections. Mrs. Burkett read it at night and made suggestions in the margins. One day after school, she asked Cecil Ryland, a student, to do a favor for her.

"I've just finished proofreading a novel by one of my former students," she said. "Would you run it over to her house?"

Cecil agreed. Later, he retold the incident.

"I gathered up the manuscript in an old stationery box, and took it and went knocking on her door. Nelle Harper Lee came to the door, and I said, 'Here's your book.' And she said 'Thank you.' Little did I realize that I held a little bit of history in my hands."

It took two and a half years of rewriting. Finally, the book was finished. Once again, the title came up. Rather than being called *Atticus,* Nelle decided to choose the title from one of the things Atticus said in the book:

"Mockingbirds don't do one thing but make music for us to enjoy. They don't eat up people's gardens, don't nest in corncribs, they don't do one thing but sing their hearts out for us. That's why it's a sin to kill a

mockingbird."

Nelle's first novel was finally complete.

To Kill a Mockingbird was scheduled for publication by J.B. Lippincott to be released in July, 1960.

Since publication, To Kill a Mockingbird *has been published with many different covers. Here are two of them.*

Chapter 14

TRUMAN CAPOTE WROTE A NICE COMMENT to go on the published copy of Nelle's book:

Someone rare has written this very fine first novel, a writer with the liveliest sense of life, and the warmest, most authentic humor. A touching book, and so funny, so likeable.

Nelle delighted in his kind words, yet she remembered the caution Ms. Hohoff offered.

"I have seen too many young hopefuls crushed by rejection. Don't be surprised, Nelle, if you sell only two thousand copies—or less. Most books by first-time novelists do," she warned.

Nelle wasn't prepared for the event that was about to change her life.

On March 3, 1960, an unexpected spring snowstorm hit New York City. Blankets of snow enveloped the city. Traffic snarled. Telephone lines were dead. The "city that never sleeps" seemed almost at a standstill. As Nelle peered from the window of her apartment, her mind wasn't on the snowstorm. Her mind still reeled from the news she'd received a few days earlier.

"Nelle, are you sitting down?" Maurice Crain chuckled when she answered. Without waiting for a reply, he said, "Have I ever got news for you! Your book has been chosen as a selection by *Reader's Digest* Condensed Books *and* the Literary Guild."

Both publications were great honors in the early 1960s. Plus, they pretty much assured that a book would be a big seller.

Nelle was speechless.

However, after having a few days to digest the news from Maurice, Nelle decided she must go to his office to show her appreciation.

Once the snowstorm passed, she bundled up in her warmest coat and set out for the Eighty-sixth Street subway stop. As she crossed Lexington Avenue, her mind still reeled from the news. She paid no attention to the route to Mr. Crain's office, for it was a familiar one. A shrill police whistle startled her.

Looking up into the harsh wind, she realized the policeman was pointing at her.

"Yes sir?" she asked politely.

"You just walked against the light," he stated.

"Didn't you hear the cars?"

"What cars?" Nelle asked.

The policemen looked at her suspiciously and then made her recite her name and address. Finally, he wrote her a ticket and ripped it from his pad.

"Be careful!" he cautioned.

Nelle stuffed the ticket in her pocket and hurried on her way. At Mr. Crain's office, he and his wife, Annie Laurie, were there to greet her. Nelle joyfully read the introduction that the editor of the Literary Guild had written about her book. The three friends toasted Nelle's good fortune and talked about her future.

A few hours later, Nelle headed home. Unbelievable thoughts went through her mind about what was happening. She could hardly wait to write to friends and relatives about everything.

Just as Nelle crossed an intersection, she heard someone call out, "Come here, lady!"

She looked up to see the angry red face of the same policeman.

"Are you deaf?" he snarled.

"No, sir," she answered quietly.

"Can you hear car horns?" he asked.

"Yes, sir, I'm sorry I'm a little distracted today," Nelle tried to explain.

The policeman didn't want explanations. He wrote her a second ticket!

A few days later, her phone rang. It was Mr. Crain.

"Are you sitting down?" he repeated. "Because I've just hung up the phone, and guess what? Annie Laurie's instincts are right about Hollywood. On top of everything else, I've just received a call—"

"NO!" Nelle stopped him. "Don't even tell me yet! Wait until I get across that intersection."

That was just the beginning of the success story of

Nelle and movie maker Alan Pakula during filming of To Kill a Mockingbird.

To Kill a Mockingbird.

To date, the book has sold over 30 million copies and is required reading for many high school students. It was made into a movie starring Gregory Peck in 1962. The movie won three Oscar Awards, the highest honor given in Hollywood. One quote from Atticus was spoken exactly as it appears in the book. It was one of 400 film quotes nominated by the American Film Industry for its *100 Years... 100 Movie Quotes.* Many times, when people remember reading the book, this is the line they most recall:

"First of all," he said, "if you can learn a simple trick, Scout, you'll get along a lot better with all kinds of folks. You never really understand a person until you consider things from his point of view—"

"Sir?"

"—until you climb into his skin and walk around in it."

Suddenly, Nelle Harper Lee, the quiet girl from Monroeville, Alabama was famous.

Requests for interviews and book signings flooded in. Lippincott, her publishing company, received sacks of fan mail addressed to "Harper Lee."

Truman Capote noted, "Poor thing—she is nearly demented: she says she gave up trying to answer her 'fan mail' when she received 62 letters in one day. I wish she could relax and enjoy it more; in this profession it's a long walk between drinks."

Nelle was interviewed in 1964 by Roy Newquist, host of the radio program "Counterpoint" as well as a critic for *The New York Post*.

"What was your reaction to the novel's enormous success?" he asked.

"Well, I can't say that it was one of surprise," Nelle answered. "It was one of sheer numbness. It was like being hit over the head and knocked cold. You see, I never expected any sort of success with *Mockingbird*. I didn't expect the book to sell in the first place."

Then, she continued, "I was hoping for a quick and merciful death at the hands of reviewers, but at the same time I sort of hoped that maybe someone would like it enough to give me encouragement. Public encouragement. I hoped for a little, as I said, but I got rather a whole lot, and in some ways this was just about as frightening as the quick, merciful death I'd expected."

"Are you working on another novel at present?" Newquist asked.

"Yes, and it goes slowly, ever so slowly," Nelle replied. "I like to write. Sometimes I'm afraid that I like it too much because when I get into work I don't want to leave it....It's strange, but instead of hating writing, I love it too much."

"I want to do the best I can with the talent God gave me," Nelle said, ending the interview. "I hope to goodness that every novel I do gets better and better...In other words all I want to be is the Jane Austen of south Alabama."

Nelle Harper Lee never had a second novel published. For years, people have wondered why she didn't. Some say that she wrote about what she knew and what she loved, and then she was done. Others say that maybe her job was complete in one book.

As the years passed, Nelle shied further from the spotlight. She declined to give interviews or to speak at public events. Some people said she'd become a 'recluse' or loner. That wasn't who Nelle had become. It was who she was all along. People had mocked her for being different all of her life. She didn't need publicity to make her happy. She'd written a Pulitzer Prize winning novel and, for her, perhaps that was enough.

Perhaps she was describing herself in the now-famous quote from the book:

If you just learn a single trick, Scout, you'll get along a lot better with all kinds of folks. You never really understand a person until you consider things from his point of view... Until you climb inside of his skin and walk around in it.

Nelle Harper Lee was who she was, and she seems happy inside her own skin. She spends most of her time in Monroeville, Alabama with some visits to New York. The town of Monroeville is proud of Nelle Harper Lee and proud to help protect her privacy and live a quiet life. Nelle enjoys spending time with her sister, Alice, who in 1907 was in her 90s and still practices law in Monroeville.

Nelle Harper Lee remains a woman of few words and mostly avoids public appearances. On August 20, 2007, she was present at the Alabama Academy of Honor ceremony in Montgomery. At the end of the ceremony, Tom Carruthers, chairman of the Academy, joked that he knew Harper Lee had something she wanted to say to the crowd.

After a brief pause, Harper Lee said, “Well, it’s better to be silent than to be a fool.” The audience burst out laughing and gave Harper Lee a standing ovation.

Epilogue

MOST READERS OF THIS BOOK will not yet have read *To Kill a Mockingbird* because parts of it are written for older people. However, the readers of this book will relate well to the fact that school teachers tell them to "write about what they know." At the beginning of each school year, teachers ask students to write narratives, or stories, about their own lives. Nelle Harper Lee was a master of using people and places that she knew to create her famous book that has never been out of print since it was published in 1960.

In the second chapter of her book, Nelle spied on her older neighbors, Captain and Mrs. Powell Jones. Mrs. Jones often yelled out to Nelle from her porch. Later, when Nelle wrote her famous book, it was easy to recognize where she got the character of Mrs. Dubose.

When Scout was well into second grade, she and Jem had moved beyond harassing Boo Radley and had grown more interested in the actual town of Maycomb.

The only problem was that to get to town, they had to pass the home of Mrs. Henry Lafayette Dubose, who lived two doors down. She was a mean old woman who always yelled terrible things at Scout and Jem. She lived alone with only a colored girl who took care of her, and the part of the day that she didn't spend in bed, she spent wrapped in shawls in a wheelchair on her front porch. It was rumored among the town that she kept a Confederate pistol hidden under those shawls, but no one knew for certain. No matter how they tried to handle Mrs. Dubose, she was always cross and mean to them, and Atticus told them to ignore it because she was just a sick, old lady.

Also, in the same chapter in this book, Jane Hybart Rosborough recalled the school's agricultural parade. In *To Kill a Mockingbird*, Nelle remembered the event as well:

My costume was not much of a problem. Mrs. Crenshaw, the local seamstress, … took some chicken wire and bent it into the shape of a cured ham. This she covered with brown cloth, and painted it to resemble the original. …She did a fine job. Jem said I looked exactly like a ham with legs. There were several discomforts, though: It was hot, it was a close fit; if my nose itched I couldn't scratch, and once inside, I could not get out of it alone.

In the fifth chapter of this book, Nelle and Truman spent a lot of time spying on the Boulware home and looking for Alfred, Jr. or "Son" who never came outside after he got in trouble for breaking into a Monroeville drugstore. Son will live in hearts for years to come because of the writing of Nelle Lee. She used him as the idea for her character, Arthur "Boo" Radley in *To Kill a Mockingbird.*

In the sixth chapter of this book, Nelle spent a lot of time playing word games at home with her father. Early in *To Kill a Mockingbird*, the daughter, nicknamed *Scout*, is told by her teacher that her father doesn't need to teach her to read at home. The teacher feels that is something Scout should learn at school. That night, Scout was upset about what the teacher had said.

"Something wrong, Scout?"

I told Atticus I didn't feel very well and didn't think I'd go to school any more if that was all right with him.

Atticus sat down in the swing and crossed his legs. His fingers wandered to his watchpocket. He said that was the only way he could think...

Bit by bit, I told him the day's misfortunes. "—and

she said you taught me all wrong, so we can't ever read any more, ever. Please don't send me back, please sir."

Atticus stood up and walked to the end of the porch. When he completed his examination of the wisteria vine he strolled back to me.

"First of all," he said, "if you can learn a simple trick, Scout, you'll get along a lot better with all kinds of folks. You never really understand a person until you consider things from his point of view—"

"Sir?"

"—until you climb into his skin and walk around in it."

Recent photo of Nelle congratulating To Kill a Mockingbird *essay contest winners (University of Alabama photo).*

Nelle Harper Lee

1926 Born on April 28

1931 Met Truman Capote

1944-45 Attended Huntingdon College in Montgomery Alabama

1948 Left for Oxford, England to participate in summer program for exchange students

1949 Moved to New York and worked as an airline reservation clerk

1956 Took a year off from work to write full time

1957 Submitted manuscript for *To Kill a Mockingbird* to J.B. Lippincott. Spent 2 1/2 years rewriting.

1959 Accompanied Truman Capote to Holcomb, Kansas to help research his famous non-fiction book *In Cold Blood*

1960 *To Kill a Mockingbird* released for publication on July 11. This book has not been out of print since that date.

1961 Won the Pulitzer Prize for *To Kill a Mockingbird* on April 12

1962 Movie *To Kill a Mockingbird* released Dec. 26. Won three Oscar Awards

1966 Named by President Lyndon B. Johnson to National Council for the Arts in June

1979 Grants no requests for further interviews or public appearances

1983 Began a non-fiction book. It was never published.

1993 Took part in the Alabama History and Heritage Festival in Eufaula. Her essay "High Romance and Adventure" was printed in the festival's papers.

1995 35th Anniversary Edition of *To Kill a Mockingbird* published September 12

2001 Inducted into the Alabama Academy of Honor

2002 Alabama Humanities Award recipient

2006 Attended Essay Contest sponsored by the Honors College at The University of Alabama on January 27

Wrote a rare letter for publication in the July edition of Oprah Winfrey's *O Magazine* on May 7

Accepted honorary degree from University of Notre Dame on May 21

Charles Shield's unauthorized biography, *Mockingbird*, published

Nelle Harper Lee with Thorsby High School senior Adrianne Farris, named in January 2007 as state winner of the essay contest (University of Alabama photo).

About the Author

Roz Morris has taught students from preschool through eighth grade. She currently teaches third grade at Shades Mountain Elementary School in Hoover, Alabama where she was named Teacher of the Year in 1994 and again in 2006. Mrs. Morris holds an M.Ed. in Elementary Education from the University of Georgia, and is certified to teach grades K through 9. She is coordinator of The Novel in the Classroom, a program designed to train teachers to write and professionally publish novels with their classroom students. Currently, more than 30 teachers in Alabama have successfully completed class novels.

Her favorite book is *To Kill a Mockingbird.*